VISION BOARD CLIP ART BOOK

HEALTH LIFE GOALS & HOME

volume 2

450+ ELEMENTS

FUTURISTA INK

★ ★ ★ ★ ★

Please leave us a review!

Join the Futurista VIP program!
Scan the code and receive **A FREE Vision Board Planner**
when you sign up to be a Futurista VIP. You'll be the first
to know about new listings and shop announcements
and you'll recieve 20% off all purchases in our Etsy Shop.

FREE! 12 steps to put you on the path to powerful manifestation!

DON'T FORGET TO CHECK OUT *Volume 1*
Fun and colorful photos, illustrations & affirmations.
A great gift for teens!

manifest

HEALTH
Fitness, Nutrition, Wellness, Self Care

LIFE GOALS
Education, Career,
Love, Marriage, Family

HOME LIFE
Your Dream House, Interior Design,
Organization, Holiday Decor

HEALTH
and
WELLNESS

I AM GRATEFUL
FOR MY BODY

I RESPECT MY BODY

I FEEL GOOD
IN MY BODY

I AM GETTING
BETTER EVERY DAY

I HAVE
ABUNDANT ENERGY

I AM HAPPY
& HEALTHY

I LIVE A HEALTHY
LIFESTYLE

I NOURISH MY BODY

I SLEEP WELL

MY BODY IS
HEALTHY & STRONG

I AM HEALED

MY BODY IS ALWAYS
WORKING FOR ME

I AM STRONG

I AM MORE
THAN MY BODY

IT IS OKAY TO SAY NO.

I ENJOY EATING
NUTRITIOUS FOODS

MY BODY IS A
POWERFUL HEALER

I DESERVE TO RELAX.

BALANCED MEALS
CAN BE SIMPLE

I AM BALANCED

I AM ENOUGH

S.T.R.O.N.G.E.R.

T.H.A.N.

Y.E.S.T.E.R.D.A.Y.

DONT
COMPARE
YOURSELF
TO
OTHERS

IM DOING
THIS
FOR ME

YOU
ARE
EQUAL

Wake
UP
Work
OUT!

BE STRONG
BE FEARLESS
BE YOU

NOW
OR
NEVER.

NEVER
GIVE UP

YOU ARE
STRONG

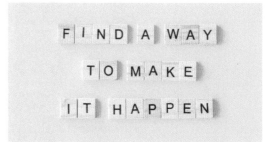

FIND A WAY
TO MAKE
IT HAPPEN

KEEP
TRYING

YOU GOT THIS

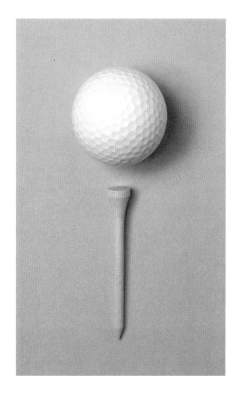

GOOD
HEALTH
IS THE
BEST
WEALTH

YOU ARE
GOOD
ENOUGH

SHINE YOUR OWN LIGHT

♥ BUT FIRST COFFEE

**BE A BETTER
YOU FOR YOU**

**MAKE IT
A LIFESTYLE,
NOT A DUTY**

**GOOD
VIBES**

TAKE
A
CHILL
PILL

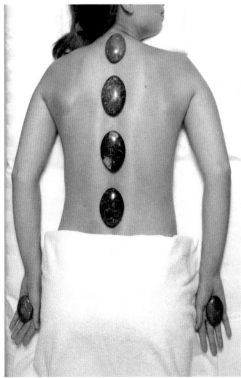

LESS
IS
MORE

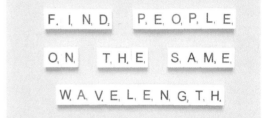

F. I. N. D. P. E. O. P. L. E.
O. N. T. H. E. S. A. M. E.
W. A. V. E. L. E. N. G. T. H.

DREAM

IT

WILL BE

OKAY

CAFFÈ FRED

CAFFÈ LUNG

CAFFÈ CORRET

AMERICANO

MACCHIATO

AFFOGAT

SELF
LOVE
IS THE
GREATEST
MEDICINE

BE GOOD
BE HAPPY
BE YOURSELF

SELF
CARE
ISN'T
SELFISH

LIFE
GOALS

I DESERVE REAL &
AUTHENTIC LOVE.

MARRIAGE IS MY GOAL
AND I AM READY IT.

I AM UNSTOPPABLE.

I AM CONFIDENT
IN MY ABILITIES

I POSSESS
ENDLESS POTENTIAL.

I AM POWERFUL

WHAT I WANT IS
WITHIN MY REACH.

MY BODY IS ABLE
TO CREATE &
SUSTAIN LIFE.

I AM CAPABLE OF
ACHIEVING MY GOALS.

OUR FAMILY IS
A PLACE OF PEACE
& HARMONY.

I AM WORTHY
OF SUCCESS.

I MOVE BOLDLY
TOWARD MY DREAM

I AM COMMITTED TO
REACHING MY GOALS.

EVERYTHING IS
POSSIBLE FOR ME

LOVE IS MY PRIORITY.

GREAT JOBS
ARE FINDING ME

I AM A POWERFUL
MANIFESTOR

I AM BLESSED
& ABUNDANT

I AM FOCUSED
& CONSISTENT

DON'T
IGNORE
YOUR
OWN
POTENTIAL

Great
IDEAS

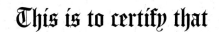
MBA
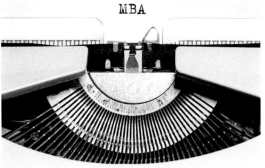

This is to certify that

has successfully completed studies
prescribed for the degree of

at

Upon recommendation of the faculty and by
authority of the Council of Trustees has been
granted, as evidence thereof, this Diploma.

@ GIRL BOSS

DON'T WAIT FOR
OPPORTUNITY
CREATE IT

Boss
Lady

DONT
SHRINK
YOURSELF
IN ORDER
TO MAKE
OTHERS
COMFORTABLE

LIVE
WHAT
YOU
LOVE

LET
YOUR
HEART
SING

LOVE IS LOVE

PARTNER

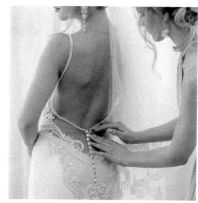

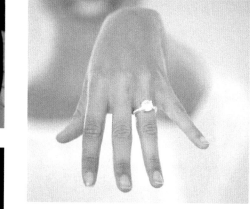

Boy or Girl?

GIRL

BOY

HERE
COMES
A BRAND
NEW
LITTLE
BABY

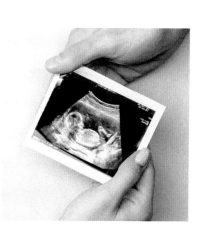

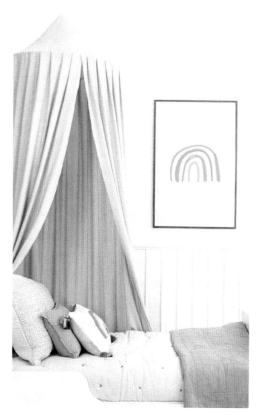

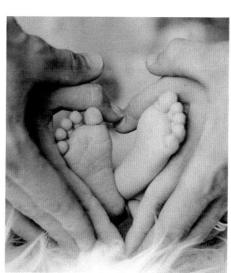

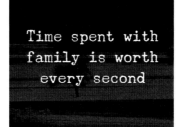

Time spent with family is worth every second

every moment matters

HOME
LIFE

EVERYTHING WILL
HAPPEN AT THE
RIGHT TIME

A BEAUTIFUL HOUSE
IS IN MY FUTURE

THE SEARCH FOR MY
HOME IS A JOYFUL
OPPORTUNITY

WE DESERVE THE
PERFECT HOME

I DO NOT WORRY
ABOUT WHAT IS
BEYOND MY CONTROL

I WILL FIND THE
PERFECT HOME

I AM GETTING CLOSER
TO OWNING A HOUSE

FINDING MY
NEW HOME IS AN
ADVENTURE

MY DREAM HOME IS
BECOMING A REALITY

EVERYTHING WORKS
OUT WELL FOR ME

I AM EAGER TO SEE
MY NEW HOME

MY PERSEVERANCE
BRINGS MY DREAMS
INTO REALITY

OUR HOME WILL
NURTURE US

I WILL FIND MY DREAM
HOME ANY MINUTE NOW

I AM PEACEFUL &
HAPPY AS I SEARCH
FOR MY NEW HOME

OUR NEW HOME
IS PART OF OUR
ABUNDANT LIFE

HOME
sweet
HOME

MY
SWEET
HOME

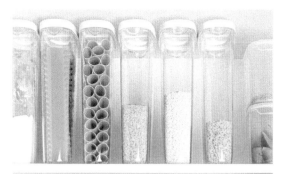

OWN
LESS
LIVE
MORE

CURRY POWDER

CORIANDER SEEDS
SPICE

HAPPY NEW YEAR

START

NEW YEAR

KISS

2025

You are *strong* and *capable* ♡

BE YOU

Do all things with love

I was there for *myself* when no one else was.

IT ALWAYS SEEMS IMPOSSIBLE UNTIL IT IS DONE

TO FIND YOURSELF THINK FOR YOURSELF

be the best version of you ♡

PRETTY THINGS INSIDE

BE STRONGER THAN YOUR EXCUSES

YOU BECOME WHAT YOU BELIEVE

GIRL POWER

ADVENTURES ARE THE BEST WAY TO LEARN

ALWAYS BELIEVE IN YOURSELF

LIFE IS BEAUTIFUL

READY FOR TAKE OFF...

DONT QUIT

DO SOMETHING GREEN TODAY

I AM CREATING THE LIFE OF MY DREAMS

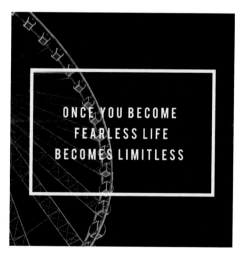

ONCE YOU BECOME FEARLESS LIFE BECOMES LIMITLESS

REMEMBER STOP THINKING ABOUT HIM

POSITIVE MIND POSITIVE VIBES POSITIVE LIFE

SAVE THE PLANET SAVE THE EARTH

Made in the USA
Las Vegas, NV
28 November 2024

12853143R00052